Norma Cole's rigorously spare poem sequence is a lyric like no other today, charming its listeners not to sleep but toward a principled wakefulness. Compressed poems bristle with tensions between language and form, precision and abstraction, lyrical affect and flat critique of a systematic claim of distance ("elsewhere") from incidents of harm. Cole's elegies, laments, and invocations deliver a "gentle summons" against an "implicated garland of/ witnesses" and "bodies of/ knowledge/ resisting a solution." A beautiful, simmering provocation, *Alibi Lullaby* challenges and enchants through the deep, dark night of our contemporary day.

—Kimberly Alidio, author of *Teeter*

Formal permutations, microshifting syllables, hastened, conjoined, and reconstituted sonicscapes undergird *Alibi Lullaby*. The presence of the multiply heard/seen/felt/touched in Norma Cole's work pluralizes the sensorium. She acutely observes cultural and political ossifications. *Alibi Lullaby* attends the evidence and residue of the social and historical event whether here/elsewhere, everyday minutiae, prosodical vulnerability and verve, geopolitical strife—the registers of tenderness and suffering.

—Myung Mi Kim, author of *Civil Bound*

Alibi is elsewhere, and lullabies draw us near. As with much of Norma Cole's work over the years, the space between is where music exists, where our songs, our indeterminate attention, find their potentialities. The songs in this book are where our world, in all of its fractured hallucinations, oscillates with the hopefulness of some other, less brutal realities. And it is here, in the incantatory music of hope, of the possible, that we are sung into with these poems. For all the darkness that looks to bleed us apart, the language issuing from these pages guides us to be near. Celan once told us that there are songs still to be sung beyond mankind. Here, we have them.

—Jerrold Shiroma, Editor of duration press

In the poem, "Rainy Day," Norma Cole writes: "monuments exist like moments." Cole recognizes the impermanence of all things, the broken and breaking state we live in, and often try to ignore. She knows the measures by which we locate ourselves in the world (and discourse) have been tampered with, removed, overturned, blotted out, supplanted by lies, and nostalgia for an age that never existed. Cole knows it is happening to everyone, everywhere. A noted translator and accomplished visual artist, she is acutely attuned to the intricate shifting relationship of image, sound, and meaning, as attested to by the title of her book, *Alibi Lullaby*. The broken lines and ruptured thoughts bring us the news: "leaping rhythm/continued arithmetic/ pulse. She knows false attempts at communication when she hears it: "he talks/blocks." The sounds emanating from these powerful poems is our collective heart. The meanings, and there are many, arise out of our well-founded anxiety. Inhabitant of a shattered world that is disintegrating further, she asks if we "fall under the apprehension/of seeing and looking away." It is the single most pressing question of our time.

—John Yau, author of *Tell It Slant*

ALIBI LULLABY

Cover design by Jeff Pethybridge
Cover typeface: Myriad Pro
Cover photo: "Hubble Views Cosmic Dust Lanes"
https://science.nasa.gov/image-detail/hubble-ngc4753-potw2420a-2/
Lenticular Galaxy NGC 4753
May 12, 2024
Credits: ESA/Hubble & NASA, L. Kelsey

Interior design by Laura Joakimson
Interior typeface: Avenir Next and Elena Basic

Library of Congress Cataloging-in-Publication Data

Names: Cole, Norma, author.
Title: Alibi lullaby / Norma Cole.
Description: Oakland, California : Omnidawn Publishing, 2025. | Summary: "Alibi,
in Latin, meant "elsewhere." Lullaby, from *lull*, to soothe, and *bye*, near, close by,
has universal elements from all cultures, "the ancient intel," songs more ancient
than thought, already fully formed when writing first occurs on clay tablets.
Now, as then, there is the framing of formal patterns and rhythms, the peaceful,
hypnotic quality, and elements of terror, turbulence, violence, the unreachable
moving frontier of "thrill, dread, uncertainty." Sun, rain, dreams, and "recent
events" – heart sounds, the spectral elegance of blood flow, murmur of melody,
fundamental patterns as well as unusual beats. A poetry of formal freefall,
looking forward while holding up the shifting mirror of memory, ALIBI LULLABY is
montage on the edge, measured with heart and pain songs. Sounds of summer,
massacres, "empathy through distress," what is life now? "I don't know (*nescio*)."
Energy, suspense, fragility – the real in words – "like writing on the wall."
-- Provided by publisher.

Identifiers: LCCN 2024055722 | ISBN 9781632431622 (trade paperback)
Subjects: LCGFT: Poetry.
Classification: LCC PR9199.3.C585 A78 2025 | DDC 811/.54--dc23/
eng/20241122
LC record available at https://lccn.loc.gov/2024055722

Published by Omnidawn Publishing, Oakland, California
www.omnidawn.com
10 9 8 7 6 5 4 3 2 1
ISBN: 978-1-63243-164-6

ALIBI LULLABY

Norma Cole

Omnidawn Publishing
Oakland, California
2025

For Robert Kaufman

Little one, who dwelt in the house of darkness –
well, you are outside now, have seen the light of the sun.
Why are you crying, why are you yelling?

Akkadian Lullaby
[Old Babylonian Period, 1950 – 1530 B.C.]

Contents

Take a Look

Take history
Take power

At no point sufficient
Accident of memory

The common truth
Conditions of visibility

Unstable orbits
Explain nothing

In the history
Of contestation

Truth cure—it's a start
Unfit for use

Nescio, not knowing
Task or matter

Insufficient uncertainties
Pose limits of understanding

The commission
Memory itself

Night Market

Rock or tree, inflexion
of tree, wild asparagus

and watercress, weeping
and leaving, parting and

fleeing, atmosphere
as always the distance

when the sun was still
shining, scattering

ardor, a metal form
straight as a cypress

useful and unnecessary
single or double, green

or variegated, sensation
recording upheaval, desertion

or deception to protect
a love, lore on a tablet

the song a minimal grammar,
walls, bridges, cement could

take the weight, lamentations
a fire, the easy kill in the night

With a Line

measure how silence
sits on the ground

the same rills, clay tablets,
gravel and stones, frozen

moments measure displacement
consequence the records of

common consent, displacement
sugar pills killing time now or

how the most euphonious cadence
a reed stylus, rosewater and

mint, the slope, distortion
meaning stay safe, tenderness

the fleeting constraints, sites
of conscription expanding

meeting control at the site
of precipitous inquiry

could it take the weight of
a frozen moment

Lull to Sleep

jump the waitlist
the concrete divider
paired gratuitous and
like cement a mistake

no sugar sang the lament
no composer of intricate
attention where looping
ancients connect unsettling

impact no longer
relevant active forgetting
making decisions
like recent events

shifts delayed or
ordinary clipboard history
a distinguishing
pressure cooker system

of keys binding directly
not direct despite
unsettling precision
but later observable

not really the sun's
expanding takeaway
real intention intentional
the giveaway of ordinary

inflexion or pained
apprehension attention
not observable fleeting
highway tension similar
empathy through distress

As Told By

position decisions
friendly equivocation

key or knife
disconcerting

concert disc
offering rose petals

the breaking
cake or praise

We should do something
blank panes

of leaded glass
maelstrom

kickback
iron from the sky

still warning
this folding

decisions
a leaflet

Your Order

is confirmed
implicated

garland of
witnesses

a kind
of control

like working
a reduction

of uncertainty
bodies of

knowledge
resisting a solution

stabbing practice
look

at the remainder
a little more

lit
courting the crystals

Like Any Body

implicated garland of
witnesses

devolution, foliage
in red

damage
no mystery

truce
a garland of wool

intention
the something else

to replace it

passage or message
carrying every body

leaning against
this same sun

more dangerous
leaving, speaking

this same sun
dreaming

See the Light

not the means
like a   small wave
in motion

you can't see
when you
look
peculiar
energy behaviors
revolution without
traits
   without
the past

ground into dust
contradictory
resolutions
          present
together (superposition)
see the inference

looks like a
proposition
makes sense

will make
a case of
interference
as of yet
inhabiting

not
gesturing
limits
of nostalgia
extended dissolves
like writing

on the wall
little mother fucker

A Scattering

open

       across

a condition of
survival

harmonic device
inner life
the instrument

and this is the
image of articulation
protect it

show it
the exact location
overlooking

a tree
any distant planet
exact conditions

alibi = elsewhere
mirages claim a piece
of evidence

images remember
the cadence
think of others

Gentle Summons

                        illusion

urgency
            agency

outside the lines
can you hear me?

things themselves
unfinished
as children

encounter
in the ledger
can you erase hunger?

dust shot on the ridge
fell for it
in alignment

light hitting the plant
bomb or leaf?
fusion jumps to conclusion
fall under the apprehension
of seeing and looking away

Occasional Placeholder

attention divided
consonant pitch

entrain to the sounds
that surround

weaving and spinning
the amulets

limbs of memories
the doves are coming

at the station
a taxi

the doves, a kite
caught in the

power lines
the bridge in a fog

and the community
of listeners disappears

reflection speaking indirectly
from the force of the sound

sensation displaced in
the voice of another

address stands in
for scriptless gesture

On the Block

don't look up
evidence exists
when stars appear
played out
before daybreak

take a history test
give it up
shrapnel   grapes
not given in advance
through their own weight

who says these words
records indicate
the glittering light
exceeds the framework
unbolted   unparalleled

the everyday mysteries
express the missing years
bound to
in excess
pretend to know

Returns, Remains

while we sleep
records pretend
tangible nothing

to know
to explain
not to reclaim

an occasion to discover
base camp is thought
office of questions or concerns

special measures dare to
return to dare
to look for

rough risks
by early afternoon
when stars appear

nothing to explain
but state sponsored
special measures

Toy Weather

making marks, condensation
revising end note

flammable vapor
everybody knows

no special effects
pitch and slope

containment defines
the field, the density

distinct, the interval
contends or amends

the question without
obvious explanation

Night Watch

rearrange
the disturbance itself
in the field
the night, the baby

whom should I send?
the question don't fit
the dropped stitch
it needed to go

forgotten lament
the baby itself
no compass
but cement itself
the chosen agent

Tension

between intricate attention
the spot through distress
of the crowd

concrete dividers, streamers
of ordinary empathy
intention intentionally

lulls suggestion to sleep
unsettling precision, real
despite conscious awareness

On the Sensations of Tone

framework ruefully
moving forward
tied notes

echo memory
hyperformed melody
out of phase

boughs resting nightly
by chance or
edge of destiny

take a book for instance
melody incomplete
inexact or paradise

the last to know
accuracy a moment
or the last to know

faceless hourglass
accuracy the hidden
voice later revealed

embodied sound
a certainty no
veiled certainty

unveiled acousmatic
sound speaking through
a reed, rivers

and canals, spectral
heart sounds, dance
in a net, stagger

for measure
the messenger
rizz up, logic

reduced, the index
of undoing of
narrative when

human and nonhuman
sound worlds meet
seized by magic

and heart grass
and pain song
contagion, tension

between order and
disorder, conjurations
open questions

later revealed
the unreachable frontier
thrill, dread, uncertainty

Rainy Day

restricted extremities during thought flight
sensitive documents: the market, the fire

like weather balloons in gear
or a plate glass window in the pavement

monuments exist like moments
such as not not measuring the world

by measuring bananas, bankrolled
by measuring the madrigals, the vivid contests

that could have been avoided by
burrowing spiral galaxies, bananas or banners

each one measuring a dollar, a wish
fishing for exits, resting or resisting

Interludes*

with the affection
of days of undetermined
significance

vaguer than a throw of the
net or scrambled
eggs

a child of the blockade
in perpetuity is not, it's
not

biography—substitution
and addition the modern
thrill

doesn't explain partly collision
—howdy, where's the
transport

the sun is trapped, puzzled
attached, attacked by its own
script

it all comes down
to this hangover of
escape

*"philosophy of acceptance," Claudio Magris

Untitled

rex block situates
north of verification

filters & high pressure
sink hole through which

little angels with little wings
winglets, the ancient intel

perpetuates sound
time circles early

rising steadily
next to nothing

melancholy architecture
add the flowers

negative overabundance
timeless problem

magnitudes, public access
and the flowers

stand revealed
by the repeated figure

Dream House Waffles

broadly speaking
when the sun is silent

self-contradicting
moves through paper

what keeps the trouble
accidents, resistance

with time
note for note

fell out
with the grappling hook

of a rage bound special
master, broadly speaking

delaying sleep
to survive

negative magnitudes
said the philosopher

No Account Syllables

no account
sound

I mean
wall

the heart
each

wall meaning
done

no nothing
voices

add bodies
uncertain

would without
compare

je have never seen you like this

tiny hand
money

the darker
room

he talks
blocks

of space
and

books of
time

I think
your

hand on
paper

least exercise
leaves

follows geographic
reduction

wait be
seen

applied against
two

images night
moves

all calm
around

the body
tell

you sometimes
no

using mouth
tonight

and no
sound

of syllables
mad

woven gestures
generate

liquid not
belonging

to me

[after "SANS AUCUN BRUIT DE SYLLABES," from *Une Méthode
descriptive*, Claude Royet-Journoud]

Illumination

standard deduction
evidence in context
action unwinding
meaningless action
hunched over
to refuse so far
to record and still
contemplate
incomplete
windlass
suspended
suspense
implicit evidence
order deactivate
not the light
we did

Mum's the Word

saturation not able inside the magnitudes
scorpion suppression oppression falling failing
oblivious silent objects

Mum's the Word

silent objects
saturation not able
inside the magnitudes
suppression, oppression
falling, failing
oblivious

The Matter

The chatter of the world is just a breath
Dante, *Purgatorio*

Conditions in the moment
conditions in the present moment
conditions are melting in the present moment

loss in different tempi, a striking
concentration of them, in it and
of it, but when the state withdraws

from the social contract, a walking dream
the armature a striking concentration
removes system from sound

some day will mean these large scale
stained glass windows seem essential
to private time: moon in Scorpio

fallen asleep but not where you
wake up: can you place this photo
from the broken old bible? Tell us

the end and ruin everything, the pink
cloud, the ridgeline and everything
grassland, aspen groves, stand of

redwoods, trees make the light
sense of distance, prospect
everchanging feverish refraction

mind not inclined for the story's
not found here

Critical Miss

permanently
beyond chagrin

intrinsic—what is
trinsic? intervals

disbanded intrude
forging, include

effects of slowness
ritual permanently

dead or at dusk
shivering lightly

frozen dismantled
aside brushed

and tarnished
burnished ruthless

witness things
and their pace

include the effects
of likely shivering

the system waves
light bulbs, folding

completely empty
deactivate the lovers

a blank sheet hovers
gone expression

almost spring

Halo of Blood

oblivious to others
the same hour

apparent order
or actual order

sugar and candle
stand up

fingers of rain
walk without

contradiction
come on

witness the set
another time

Explain the Gap

between recent events
and a general theory
of conflict of interest
lost in the span
anything other than
embodied force
moving outside
violet or marigold
where's the grass
incomplete memory
as past predicament
potential in question
quiet as stone

And Nothing

like lost knowledge
a shovel, the secret hello

the soldiers, news from
the heart of the meter

blurry reconstruction
still standing on the corner

gutter lossy, the big
star formation, the chance

to understand something
like hallucinations

or power dynamics
tip over, words not meant

where massacres continue
on summer nights

Same Angel

forget to
to intercept air (with
reason?)

meditation:
one has facts
one has reason

on fire: beyond measure
a thousand years in a day
"Eerily empty roads,"
writes Brett from
a truck run

rhyming tea and moon
a checkerboard floor, those
slow-rhyming disappearing
women

how far are you
going? Questions
are beauties, systems
of control

playing
around the mouth, not
enough dreamtime
concealment the empty
order

The Sweet Hello

don't entrance
the heart of the meter
for massacres continue
on summer nights

trouble by bound
reality is the fault we
endorse let's some
ending is right now

no events the thing
like forks, spoons
words not meant today
how round things

tip over
the bowl of experience
see it or sink
when dust rules

voice off
listen, cloud, principal
asked or not
shoes to get there

islands for silence
time approaches

Islands for Silence

sooner or later, time
approaches, highly
volatile, almost asleep
and not get their footing

uncanny vault
at its valley, simple
acts, body fusion, polar
events, listen like clouds

voice off, pin up the
past, news from a porch
the heart of the meter,
the principal fault

is its ending
trip over it, mountains
of suspense, scent
of fennel in summer

mid summer nights
massacres continue
that crinkling shovel
sound, its muse or not,
the sign shaped sign,
flat as a verse

Daily Life

same attention
indeterminate
in the moment
rain with the
road grounded
to itself like
studying ink to
never settle to
stay at home
to start at home
memory a predicament
all the pages
live and looking
back, long takes
in the dark
with the book
in question

An Ordinary Evening

To act is to be committed, to be committed is to be in danger.
James Baldwin

An ordinary evening
is to be in danger

Attraction/Distraction

the fake book
a scant melody

sweet or agreeable
action: a thing done

alteration by force
to drive, to travel

coming about
on a reach

drawn to
drawn apart

Superliminal Trance

warp bubble
is impossible
the ship
in the
bubble created

from nothing
contracting in
front expanding
behind faster
than light

the ship
when dark
matter was
far too
dark to

generate a
negative energy
field but
mass deforms
spacetime total

mass many
Jupiters this
bubble resembles
a flock
of birds

rings and
disks, charged
particles experience
time at
all moments

Namaste

salutations my child
you in your heart

heard the basics
the basic first finger

the travel music
a fictional gun

the gesture of folding
romance of the exit

any hour there's
nothing imagining

history at the shore
drifting from time

to time the key here
imagination and failure

its own zeal, pretense
that starts here

drafting the key here
meaning the evidence

like us, they once
had time

LOST DANCE

Last chance

words people energies
somewhere in there
that that punctuation

recovery my spoken
moving never never
play something else

again still somewhere
and will will
be are own

grammar structure you
you moreso life
to starting starting

with say say
power just line-up
granted shows for

for not intentional
taken before enough
can one one

structure get not
not voice foolscap
rush would like

like local food
issue call to
be be what

Wherever

the
the
the the
the
the night

dreams
writing harbor
wall refugees
portraits palais
exile barge
history space
space

facts sighting history

ground crossing
spiral attraction
sail gratitude
water curtain
watch metro
clocks proposals
sites unseen
onlookers stories

of
on beyond
of from
between
of of
and a

on in
another
racing
slow
lost
run is
be told
sold

Am
want
touch
will
take
is
life's
offering

will
take
birthday
blessing

earth's
I
lost
the
my
middle
my
today

their
last
the
final
the
last
human's
I
I

my
empty
in
of love
with
friends

When

I
it
if

like
was
saw
were

filled
rising
billowing
blooming

smoke
flames
smoke

hilltops
ridge
sky

inevitable
visible
shimmering

pinks
purples
browns

not
for
gone

It where which
from of
of from

and ones which had

belonging track
feeling
carrying the the ships

learned something
about departed

kept simply

sailed fastest

eternal
mail
and and
land

When we
have said
that

it it
transmit it
is only
which does
which movements

upon those is
placed
influences
which the office of

the body, between objects
a conductor

receives and acts
to to them and

not arrest them

When important
all problems
anything very
nothing

money nothing

no no
aren't you
you able
to

have
was after you
do discover
no peaceful
transport

Taking away

it it we these
this the a
city

was had warm
had giving
alive

burying time
dangers escaped
bearing shadow
fallen

and
and

life
again

over and now

Did it say
they haven't
they keeps you

in from little
oh did you
sleeping think

what what if her
her dream up slept
let them in did wake

as at I tell all
I am no
you too

These which breeze
would break
first snow

dusk plowed
brown road
remaining

against fields of
clarity either side
on took on tomorrow

of contours all whole
showed just sharply
sloped before the

curious down a the
the landscape the wisps
the warm up up

When at
the the
world ourselves
protect
we
it
it
and world
encounter
than new
from being
it patterns

for look
it
comes

In and
of it

in it

is it

in to
by to
we to
us by
into

We by we
have

live
see
do

this is
is that
is the

see

we
process

time
something
something

and
and

Categories
so impossible

the is
classifying
complete
mutable
chaotic
creating
already
continually

rather not
not becoming
establishing
every
being
again

I
I
me
them

that
which never
could course

from feeling
remembered

mirror certain
landscapes

remembered
transformed

of carry
of nature

with paint
and become

Pattern
fraction
heart

of in
of to
of and

and that
the the
beautiful irrational

they are
they have
pure number

leaping rhythm
continued arithmetic
pulse

even the
sense
sets beat

Acknowledgements

Farber, Walter. *Magic at the Cradle: Babylonian and Assyrian Lullabies.* *Anthropos* 1990

Hellberg, Dustin. "Rhythm, Evolution and Neuroscience in Lullabies and Poetry." Academia.edu

Heartfelt thanks to the many editors, among them Micah Ballard, Garrett Caples, Kirby, Jay Labbe, Dale Smith, Paul Vogel and Nicholas Whittington.

Thanks to the Poets Tea.

Thank you to NASA for the cover photograph.

Thank you to Jeffrey Pethybridge for the cover design.

Special thanks to Omnidawn co-publishers Rusty Morrison and Laura Joakimson.

Norma Cole is the author of poetry books including *FATE NEWS*, *Win These Posters and Other Unrelated Prizes Inside*, *Where Shadows Will: Selected Poems 1988–2008*, *Collective Memory*, *Spinoza in Her Youth*, and *Actualities*, a collaboration with painter Marina Adams. *TO BE AT MUSIC: Essays & Talks* appeared in 2010. Her translations from the French include Danielle Collobert's *It Then*, *Crosscut Universe: Writing on Writing from France* (edited and translated by Cole), and Jean Daive's *White Decimal*. Cole has had poems in many literary magazines including *Gramma*, *Posit*, *Brooklyn Rail*, *Art in America*, *Hambone*, *Sulfur*, *Conjunctions*, *HOW(ever)*, *Talisman*, and *Acts*; and in anthologies such as *American Hybrid: a Norton Anthology of New Poetry*, *Best American Experimental Writing*, and *women: poetry: migration (an anthology)*. Honors include Regents' Lecturer at University of California, Berkeley, Fall 2008, and Special Guest at the Summer Writing Program, Naropa University, 2024. Awards include the Foundation for Contemporary Arts, Fund for Poetry, Gertrude Stein Awards, the Richardson Award for Non-Fiction Prose, and the Wallace Alexander Gerbode Foundation Award for Poetry. Born in Toronto, Canada, she lives in San Francisco.

Alibi Lullaby

by Norma Cole

Cover design by Jeff Pethybridge

Cover font: Myriad Pro

Interior design by Laura Joakimson

Interior typeface: Avenir Next and Elena Basic

Printed in the United States by Books International,
Dulles, Virginia on Acid Free Archival Quality Recycled Paper
Publication of this book was made possible in part by gifts from Katherine &
John Gravendyk in honor of Hillary Gravendyk,
Francesca Bell, Mary Mackey, and The New Place Fund

Omnidawn Publishing Oakland, California

Staff and Volunteers, Spring 2025

Rusty Morrison & Laura Joakimson, co-publishers

Rob Hendricks, poetry & fiction editor,

& post-pub marketing

Jeffrey Kingman, copy editor

Sharon Zetter, poetry editor & book designer

Anthony Cody, poetry editor

Liza Flum, poetry editor

Sophia Carr, production editor

Elizabeth Aeschliman, fiction & poetry editor

Jennifer Metsker, marketing assistant

Avantika Chitturi, marketing assistant

Angela Liu, marketing assistant